TIME

Turning the Hours You Have into the Life You Want

L E A P Learning Empowerment & Achieving Potential

ISBN 978-93-81115-66-4

First published in 2011 by Leadstart
A brand of One Point Six Technologies Private Limited
Unit no. 26, Ground Floor, A1, Shram Safalya,
Wadala Truck Terminal Road, Near Post Office,
Antop Hill, Mumbai -400037.
Email:info@leadstartcorp.com
www.leadstartcorp.com

Marketed & Distributed in India by Unbound Script
2/41, Ansari Road, Darayaganj, Delhi - 110002

EDITORS OF LEADSTART

The Editors of Leadstart are a team of passionate literary enthusiasts with a creative and progressive focus. Our team includes distinguished authors, researchers, contributors, in-house editors, and writing talent from around the world. Many literary projects require a diverse team rather than a single author to write or update the book. These projects often involve cases where the original author is unable to continue, whether because they are no longer available or have passed away. Our work thus spans a range of content, from original writings to thoughtfully abridged classics, updated editions, and translations.

ABOUT THE LEAP SERIES

The LEAP series of books has been conceived as a tool of empowerment for every individual to achieve their full potential.

There are certain aspirations that every person in the world shares. We all want to be happy. We all want to lead fulfilling lives. We all want to find our soulmate. We all want a job we love doing. We all want good friends who will share our joy and sorrow. We all want to believe that there is a purpose to our lives.

While the commonality of these goals spans the globe, their achievement is entirely individual. Each person possesses a unique and mixed gift of strengths and weaknesses, special talents and handicaps. To focus our individual lives on all that is positive within us, all that is possible for us to do, to be and to achieve, we need to take conscious steps towards it. The empowerment of our lives is an individual pursuit. The decisions are yours. The action is yours. To do the very best with what one has been given – that is the ultimate achievement of a life well lived.

You Are You
First, we must recognise ourselves and accept our particular basket of capabilities. Nobody is the same. Nor is it necessary to be like someone else.

Find Your Horizons
Once we are at peace with the composition of our own individuality, we can set out to enhance our capabilities in order to achieve full potential as an individual. We can utilise all the teaching around us to stretch our talents to the fullest extent to achieve worthwhile goals.

Cap The Leak
Once we recognise our potential, we can work to minimise the influence and impact of our weak points to allow the strengths to shine in everything we do.

Row Your Boat
Every day is part of the journey. Sometimes you win the day. Sometimes the day is lost. But you keep rowing towards the shore, towards your goals. In India, it is called sadhana. That special power within you drives you to achieve what you have set yourself to do.

The LEAP series teaches methods of individual empowerment.

ꙮ

CONTENTS

INTRODUCTION

The Core of Time Management

Time is the one resource that does not renew itself. It moves quietly and without pause, indifferent to our plans and emotions. Every hour spent is an exchange. Something leaves us, and something else takes its place. To manage time, therefore, is not to control the clock but to learn how to shape our experience within it. The true skill of time management is not about fitting more into your day but about aligning what you do with what truly matters. It is the art of choosing with intention, moment by moment, in a world that constantly asks for more than you can give.

Most people think of time management as a system of calendars, lists, and schedules. Those are useful tools, but they address the surface of the problem. Beneath them lies something deeper: the relationship you have with your attention, your energy, and your purpose. You can fill every hour with tasks and still feel empty at the end of the day if none of them feel meaningful. You can meet every deadline and still feel behind if your attention is scattered and your energy depleted. Managing time begins with understanding yourself: how you think, how you tire, how you recover, and how you choose what deserves your focus.

In the rush of modern life, it is easy to confuse movement with progress. We spend our days responding to messages, crossing off items from to-do lists, and multitasking between windows, all in the name of efficiency. Yet, the faster we move, the less time we seem to have. This paradox exists because time expands or contracts based on attention. When your mind is fragmented, even short tasks feel long and draining. When you are immersed in a single activity that matters, hours can pass unnoticed, and you emerge fulfilled. The goal, then, is not to manage minutes but to master presence. Attention, not the clock, determines how fully you experience time.

Every system of time management rests on three foundations: clear goals, structured priorities, and deliberate focus. Without these, every plan collapses under distraction. Setting a clear goal is not just about knowing what you want to achieve; it is about understanding why it matters. A goal without meaning is like a destination without direction. It creates motion, but there is no satisfaction. Structure helps you translate that goal into daily choices, and focus ensures that those choices stay aligned with your purpose. Together, they turn vague intention into tangible progress.

The essence of effective time use is captured in the Pareto principle, often known as the 80/20 rule. It reminds us that a small portion of our effort produces most of our results, and that most of what we do contributes very little to what we value. If you can identify the few tasks that create the greatest impact and devote your best attention to them, you multiply your effectiveness without multiplying your hours. This principle is not just a tool for productivity, but a philosophy of focus. It invites you to shift from doing more to doing what matters most.

Many people resist time management because it feels restrictive, as if planning steals spontaneity. In truth, structure is what gives freedom its shape. When you define your priorities, you are not limiting your life. You are protecting it. Time spent planning is not time wasted; it is time invested in clarity. A few minutes spent defining what truly deserves your focus can save hours of reactive effort. The goal is not to live by a rigid schedule but to create a rhythm that supports what you value most. When you know where your time goes, you begin to live deliberately instead of reactively.

Time is not simply measured in hours and minutes but in energy, attention, and meaning. You can have plenty of time and still feel exhausted if your energy is scattered. You can have a few hours but accomplish much if you use them with clarity and care. Managing time effectively means managing yourself, your mindset, your emotions, and your ability to recover. When you treat your time as a reflection of your inner state, you begin to see that improving your focus or your well-being is not separate from managing your hours; it is the foundation of it.

The modern world tempts us to believe that doing more is the same as doing well. Multitasking is celebrated, speed is rewarded, and the quiet moments of reflection are seen as inefficiency. Yet, the real power of time management lies in slowing down enough to choose with awareness. Productivity without direction leads to exhaustion. Efficiency without meaning leads to emptiness. To use time well is to give every hour a purpose that aligns with your values. It is not about filling every moment with work, but about filling your life with moments that matter.

Imagine designing your time as you would design a home. Every space has a purpose, and every choice reflects the kind of life you want to live. You would not fill every corner with furniture simply because it is available. You would choose what fits, what supports, what brings joy. Your days deserve the same care. Planning your time is not about controlling life; it is about curating it. You cannot extend the number of days you have, but you can expand their quality by living them intentionally.

The truth is that time cannot be managed; only actions within it can. The clock moves at the same pace for everyone. What separates those who thrive from those who struggle is not the amount of time they have but how consciously they use it. The question is not how much you can do in a day, but how well what you do reflects who you are and where you want to go. Each moment you spend with awareness is a moment you have fully lived.

Time management is not a life hack. It is a practice of presence. It begins with clarity, grows through discipline, and flourishes in purpose. When you stop chasing hours and start shaping them, you discover that time is not something you lose; it is something you experience. The challenge of this book is simple but profound: to help you stop surviving time and start living within it, to treat every day as both a tool and a gift.

ഗ്ര

1

THE MYTH OF BUSYNESS

Modern life glorifies the full calendar. We measure worth by output, fill our schedules to the edge, and take pride in saying that we are busy. Busyness has become a badge of honour, a modern signal of importance. Yet beneath that surface lies a deeper truth: being busy is not the same as being effective. The constant motion that fills our days often disguises a quiet absence of direction. It feels productive because it keeps us moving, but movement without clarity is motion without meaning.

Busyness feeds on fear. The fear of being left behind, of seeming idle, of not doing enough to justify our place in the world. When we stay constantly occupied, we do not have to sit with uncertainty or self-doubt. The noise of activity drowns out the discomfort of reflection. That is why it is so easy to stay in motion even when the motion leads nowhere. The mind equates action with control, and control feels safe. Yet in truth, much of what we call productivity is just avoidance dressed in efficiency. We chase tasks to escape thought. We fill the silence because stillness feels threatening.

In every industry, from creative work to corporate life, busyness has become a performance. We answer emails at midnight, multitask through meetings, and respond instantly to messages as if speed itself were a measure of value. But constant responsiveness fragments attention. Each interruption pulls a thread from your focus until the fabric of deep work begins to tear. When your day becomes a sequence of reactions, you stop choosing and start complying. You respond to what shouts loudest instead of what matters most. It results in exhaustion without actually fulfilling anything.

Busyness creates a dangerous illusion: that effort alone equals progress. We tell ourselves that as long as we are occupied, we are moving forward. But activity is not achievement. You can sprint all day on a treadmill and end up exactly where you began. What truly defines progress is not how much effort you expend but where that effort is directed. Without purpose, even the hardest work leads to fatigue instead of growth. Without reflection, even success feels hollow because you never paused to ask whether what you achieved was what you actually wanted.

The addiction to busyness often starts innocently. It feels good to be needed, to fill the day with visible tasks, to check things off a list. There is a small rush of satisfaction in every completion, a brief hit of progress that fades as quickly as it comes. Over time, this becomes a cycle. You begin to seek the feeling of completion more than the impact of the work itself. The checklist becomes the purpose. The day becomes a race to fill itself. What once felt satisfying begins to feel consuming, because you are no longer working toward something.

To break free from busyness, you must first redefine what productivity means. Productivity is not about how many hours you fill but how much meaning you create within them. A quiet hour spent in focus often yields more than a noisy day spent multitasking. The challenge is to value stillness as much as movement. Reflection, planning, and rest are not inefficiencies. They are the roots from which all effective action grows. When you pause long enough to think, you stop reacting and start choosing. You begin to shape your time instead of letting it shape you.

Start by asking yourself simple but difficult questions: What am I busy doing? Why am I doing it? What would happen if I stopped? These questions strip away the illusion of necessity that busyness creates. Often, the work that consumes our time is not the work that builds our future. It is the small, low-value noise that keeps us occupied while real priorities wait in silence. The moment you identify what truly moves you forward, you begin to see how much of your day can be reclaimed. Awareness breaks the trance of constant motion.

It also helps to notice how busyness affects your inner life. Constant rush shortens attention, heightens anxiety, and numbs the ability to feel satisfaction. When every minute is spoken for, there is no space left to enjoy the moment that is actually happening. You begin to live always in anticipation of the next task, never in the experience of the current one. Over time, this erodes presence. The mind begins to equate calm with guilt and rest with irresponsibility. Yet rest is not a break from progress; it is a condition for it. The most effective people in any field are not those who move fastest, but those who know when to stop.

Reclaiming your time begins with subtraction. Instead of asking, "What else can I do?" ask, "What can I remove?" Every unnecessary obligation cleared from your schedule returns energy to what matters. Every distraction you eliminate strengthens your focus. You do not need to overhaul your life in one grand gesture; start small. Cancel a commitment that drains you. Leave an hour unscheduled. Turn off a notification that interrupts your flow. Each act of removal is a quiet act of defiance against the myth of busyness. It is a way of saying that your time will no longer be defined by noise.

When you stop glorifying busy, you start honouring depth. You begin to realise that a meaningful day is not one packed with motion but one marked by purpose. The quality of your attention becomes the true measure of your productivity. The more present you are with what you do, the more real progress you make. Busyness scatters life into fragments; focus gathers it into coherence. The choice between the two is not about discipline alone; it is about courage. It takes courage to slow down in a world that equates slowness with failure.

The myth of busyness will always tempt you because it offers an easy substitute for significance. It feels safer to say, "I'm too busy," than to admit, "I don't know what matters most right now." But clarity begins in that admission. Once you allow yourself to pause, you gain perspective. Once you stop trying to fill every minute, you learn to experience it. The goal is not to escape work or ambition but to align them with meaning. When your time reflects your priorities, you no longer need to prove your worth by staying busy. You live it through what you choose to give your hours to.

Busyness will always whisper that faster is better. But the truth is quieter. Better is better. Clarity beats speed. Depth beats volume. Purpose beats noise. When you begin to live by these truths, your relationship with time transforms. You stop racing against it and start moving with it. And that is where real productivity begins, not in the rush, but in the rhythm of awareness.

2

MANAGING TIME EFFECTIVELY

Time is both the most democratic and the most misunderstood resource in the world. Every person receives the same twenty-four hours, yet the outcomes of those hours vary infinitely. The difference lies not in the quantity of time but in the *quality of its use.* Managing time effectively is not about squeezing every second dry. It is about directing your energy with clarity and precision, ensuring that the time you spend becomes a reflection of your highest priorities, not a reaction to your loudest distractions.

Most people treat time as something to fill; the truly effective treat it as something to *shape.* You don't manage hours; you manage focus, attention, and decision-making within those hours. Every technique in this chapter revolves around one principle: that time management is really *self-management.* The more you understand how your mind, emotions, and environment interact, the more time begins to work in your favour rather than against you.

Start With Direction

Every hour of your life asks the same question: *What will you do with me?* If you don't decide, the world will decide for you. Notifications, conversations, and half-finished tasks will fill the space, and soon your day will feel full but meaningless. The antidote is direction, knowing where you're going and why you're doing it.

Goal setting is how you define that direction. Without clear goals, even effort becomes aimless. It's like sprinting in fog, you move quickly but don't know if you're heading the right way. A clear goal is a compass. It aligns your decisions and gives your actions a sense of inevitability.

- The **SMART** framework is a simple but profound way to turn ideas into action:
- **Specific:** Define exactly what you're doing. "Finish reading Chapter 4 of my marketing textbook" beats "Study."
- **Measurable:** Know when success is reached. "Finish a 10-slide presentation draft" gives you closure.
- **Achievable:** Match ambition with realism. Goals should challenge, not crush. "Run three times this week for 30 minutes" is far more realistic as a beginner than "running a marathon".
- **Relevant:** Ensure alignment with what truly matters to you. A goal that excites you sustains focus. "Study consumer trends to support my marketing project" aligns with your coursework, whereas "Browse general business news" spreads your energy too thin.

- **Time-bound:** Create urgency with a clear boundary. Without it, time expands indefinitely. "Complete my project proposal by Friday, 6 p.m." keeps momentum alive, without a time frame, time expands indefinitely.

But SMART goals are only the surface. What truly drives action is *emotional clarity*. Ask yourself: *Why does this goal matter to me?* When meaning is missing, motivation fades. Link each goal to a value: growth, freedom, contribution, mastery. That connection turns discipline into devotion.

Example:

"I want to write one article per week because sharing ideas helps me grow as a communicator and reach people who feel stuck."

That "why" keeps you grounded when energy dips.

For bigger ambitions, build a *goal ladder*:

- **Top Rung:** Long-term vision (e.g., launch a business, finish a degree).
- **Middle Rung:** Quarterly milestones (e.g., finish course module, design prototype).
- **Bottom Rung:** Daily actions (e.g., one hour of focused study).

Each rung supports the one above it. Small actions are no longer trivial; they are the bricks of your larger purpose.

Reflection Prompt: What are your top three priorities this month, and how do your daily actions reflect them? If they don't, it's not a failure; it's a signal to realign.

Prioritise by Impact, Not Urgency

Once direction is set, the challenge becomes choosing *what to do first*. The illusion of modern productivity is that everything is urgent. Every ping, every email, every request feels like a fire to put out. But effectiveness requires separating *what is loud* from *what is important*.

The **Eisenhower Matrix** provides a clear framework:

Category	Description	Example
Urgent + Important	Immediate crises or pressing goals	Submitting a deadline project
Important, Not Urgent	Long-term, meaningful growth	Learning, planning, exercise
Urgent, Not Important	Tasks that feel pressing but don't move you forward	Replying to low-value messages
Neither	Distractions disguised as activity	Excessive social media, gossip

Spend 60–70% of your time on *Important, Not Urgent*. That i zone of mastery, where prevention replaces firefighting. That's w books are written, bodies are strengthened, and careers adv before deadlines exist.

If you live in the first quadrant, you're surviving.
If you live in the second, you're leading.

Pair this with the Pareto Principle, and 80% of your result from 20% of your activities. Identify the few things that mc biggest difference, then protect them like sacred time.

Practical ways to prioritise:

- List everything on your plate. Highlight the 3 tasks that, if done today, would matter most.
- Schedule those first when your energy is highest.
- If you can't do everything, trade quantity for significance.
- Ask: "If I could only accomplish one thing this week, what would make the most impact?"

Example:

If your goal is fitness, "Go to the gym three times a week" is more impactful than "Research ten workout routines." Action outweighs perfection.

Over time, prioritisation becomes instinctive. You'll feel it as a quiet confidence that you are doing the right work, not just staying busy.

Design Your System, Don't Just Fill It

A planner is not a list of punishments; it's a contract with your future self. You don't plan because life must be controlled. You plan so that chaos has less room to grow.

A strong time system balances *structure and fluidity.* Structure gives focus; fluidity gives resilience.

The Building Blocks of a Good System

1. **Capture:** Write down everything that demands attention. The brain is for ideas, not storage.
2. **Clarify:** Identify what's actionable. If it takes less than two minutes, do it now.
3. **Organise:** Assign time slots or categories.

4. **Review:** Check progress daily and weekly.
5. **Execute:** Focus on one thing at a time, fully and deliberately.

Many systems exist, from minimal notebooks to digital dashboards, but the best one is the one you *use consistently*. Whether you love analogue journals or clean apps, the key is rhythm. Choose tools that make starting easier, not fancier.

Example layout:

MORNING

- Top 3 Outcomes: ______________________________
- Deep Work Block (90 mins): ___________________
- Meetings / Admin: _____________________________

AFTERNOON

- Short Break (15 mins)
- Secondary Tasks / Collaboration
- Progress Review

EVENING

- Reflection: What worked? What didn't?
- Reset workspace for tomorrow

To make this system effective, include buffers between tasks. The mind doesn't switch contexts instantly. It needs a break to decompress and to prepare itself for the next task. Five minutes of breathing or standing between deep work sessions resets your focus and prevents burnout.

Time Blocking & Contextual Batching

Don't leave your hours to chance. Assign *blocks of time* for specific types of work. Group similar tasks together, emails, calls, design work, and reading, to reduce cognitive switching costs.

Example:

- 9:00–10:30: Deep project work
- 10:30–11:00: Emails and messages
- 11:00–12:30: Meetings or collaborations

Switching tasks constantly is like restarting a car engine over and over. It drains fuel. When you batch tasks by context, you build momentum instead of losing it.

Avoid the Setup Trap

Many people spend more time optimising their tools than using them. Endless reorganising of apps, planners, and dashboards is disguised procrastination. The true purpose of a system is to make action smoother. If your system takes longer to manage than the work itself, simplify it.

See Where Your Time Really Goes

The first step to mastery is measurement. Most people *guess* how they spend their time, and they're usually wrong. The reality only becomes visible when you track it.

You don't need complex software. A simple notepad, spreadsheet, or split-page journal works. For a few days, log what you *planned* to do versus what you *actually* did.

Time	Planned	Actual	Notes
8–9	Review report	Checked email	Distracted early
9–10	Write draft	Finished half	Interrupted call
10–11	Meeting	Overran	Adjusted plan

This side-by-side view reveals where intention leaks. You'll discover patterns:

- Repeated distractions at the same hour.
- Tasks that always take longer than you think.
- Windows of high energy that you aren't using fully.

Once you understand your natural rhythm, adjust your schedule around it.

Energy mapping: noting when you're most alert, creative, or reflective. Write or strategise when energy peaks; do admin or light work when it dips.

Reflection Prompt: What would happen if you gave your best two hours to your most important goal every day?

Create Systems That Work for You: No two people think alike, so no two people should plan alike. Your method should *fit your mind.*

Some principles to personalise:

Chronotype awareness: Morning larks vs. night owls. Schedule demanding work at your natural peak.

Decision fatigue: Limit the number of choices you make daily. Simplify clothes, meals, or routines so that willpower is preserved for important work.

Rituals: Anchor transitions. A cup of tea before deep work or a short walk after helps the mind shift gears.

Weekly reviews: Every week, assess what worked, what didn't, and what to change. Reflection converts chaos into learning.

Example:

If you notice that Mondays are filled with meetings and mental clutter, designate Tuesdays as "deep work days". No meetings, no shallow tasks. Protect that space fiercely. Over time, you'll build "islands of focus" within your week.

Remember, simplicity wins. A great time system feels calm and doesn't demand perfection, but promotes consistent actions and schedules.

Software Recommendations & Digital Tools

Search for:

- "Best time management apps for students"
- "Time tracking software for freelancers"
- "How to use Google Calendar for task management"
- "Distraction blocker tools for Mac/Windows"

Always test the tools yourself before committing. What works for one person may not suit your workflow or device ecosystem.

Use community-driven review sites like Reddit or YouTube walkthroughs to see how tools work in real life. And remember, no tool will work unless it fits your goals, habits, and systems.

Digital Calendars

One of the most effective time management tools is the digital calendar. Applications like **Google Calendar, Microsoft Outlook,** and **Apple Calendar** help you structure your day with clear visibility. You can:

- Schedule meetings and tasks
- Set reminders and notifications
- Block out time for focused work
- Share calendars for collaborative planning

These apps allow synchronisation across multiple devices, ensuring your schedule is always accessible. Many users find value in setting recurring events and colour-coding tasks to distinguish between personal, academic, and professional responsibilities.

Task Management Apps

Task management software helps break down your workload into manageable items. Some current popular choices include:

- **Todoist** – A powerful, minimalist app that supports labels, priorities, and recurring tasks.
- **Trello** – Ideal for visual planners, using boards, lists, and cards to organise to-dos.

- **Asana** – Popular among teams for project and task tracking.
- **Notion** – A customizable workspace that combines tasks, notes, and databases.

These tools support better organisation and allow you to create structured workflows for daily and long-term goals. Many also integrate with calendars, timers, and communication tools.

Time Tracking Software

To truly understand where your time goes, time tracking tools offer data-backed insights. Some of these apps are used quite a lot today by those attempting to manage time:

- **Toggl** – Tracks time spent on different tasks and generates reports.
- **RescueTime** – Monitors app and website usage to categorise your productivity.
- **Clockify** – Allows manual or automatic time logging and team timesheets.

Time tracking is especially useful for freelancers or remote workers who bill by the hour or want to understand where they lose focus during the day.

Your Time System in One Page

- Define three meaningful outcomes every morning.
- Write SMART goals for long-term clarity.
- Prioritise tasks using the Eisenhower Matrix.
- Focus on the top 20% that yield 80% of results.

- Use planners, time blocks, or journals to anchor focus.
- Track time to gain awareness and spot waste.
- Match work to your energy peaks.
- Simplify decisions and design rituals for flow.
- Review weekly, refine monthly.

Time management is not simply about controlling every hour. It's about understanding yourself within time and what to make of that time.. The most successful people not only work the most, but they also work with rhythm. They know when to push themselves and when they reach their limit. They also know when they must take matters into their hands and when they need to delegate their tasks, enabling them to be more efficient and increasing the amount of work they get done.

When you manage your time effectively, you're not negotiating with your day. You start leading it. You begin to live every hour with intention, proof that you are living, and not merely existing.

ഇന്ദ

3

MANAGING DISTRACTIONS IN THE AGE OF NOISE

We live in an age where attention has become the most valuable currency in the world. Companies fight for it, screens harvest it, and the constant pulse of notifications ensures that our focus is rarely our own. Modern distraction is not a sign of weakness; it is the natural by-product of an environment designed to capture and hold your gaze. Each ping, alert, and flashing banner is a small tug at the mind's limited supply of awareness, and together they form a steady erosion of presence. If time is the measure of life, then attention is its texture, i.e. the quality of your days depends not on how many hours you have, but on how consciously you live them. To manage distractions, therefore, is to reclaim control over the only truly finite resource you possess: your ability to choose what matters.

Most people imagine distraction as a battle against noise, yet the real struggle lies within. External interruptions are only half the story. The deeper form of distraction begins internally, through restlessness, uncertainty, and the subtle discomfort that arises whenever work becomes difficult. You glance at your phone not because we need it, but because it offers escape from the unease of staying with a task that demands focus. Every time you switch from one activity to another, a part of your attention lingers behind on the previous task, leaving what psychologists call *attention residue*. This residue accumulates with every shift, fragmenting your thought process until even simple tasks feel strangely effortful. The result is a culture of busyness without depth, where activity replaces progress and effort replaces clarity.

The first step toward reclaiming attention is clarity of purpose. Focus cannot survive in a vacuum; it must be attached to meaning. Before you begin a task, pause to ask yourself why it matters. A clear reason turns distraction into disinterest, and once you see the connection between effort and purpose, your brain naturally resists wandering. Meaning anchors focus in a way that sheer willpower cannot. A well-defined "why" cuts through noise better than any productivity hack. This is why the most effective people do not necessarily have stronger discipline; they have stronger reasons.

Once meaning is established, the next task is design. Distraction thrives in disorder, both mental and physical. To work deeply, you must shape your surroundings into an environment that invites concentration instead of resistance. One of the simplest ways to do this is through structured focus intervals, such as the Pomodoro Technique. You set a timer for twenty-five minutes of concentrated effort on one task, followed by a short five-minute break. After four such cycles, you take a longer rest of fifteen to thirty minutes. The genius of this system lies in its rhythm. Each timed session feels achievable, lowering the barrier to starting, while the breaks provide regular recovery that keeps your energy steady. Over time, these intervals train your mind to enter flow faster and stay there longer. You begin to associate focus with comfort rather than strain, and the boundary between effort and ease starts to dissolve.

Physical space plays a similar role in sustaining focus. The brain constantly scans its environment for signals of safety and relevance. A cluttered desk sends messages of unfinished business, forcing your mind to filter irrelevant stimuli before it can begin meaningful work. A clean, minimalist workspace tells your nervous system that it can relax, that there is nothing else demanding attention. Lighting matters more than most people realise. Bright, natural light heightens alertness, while dim or flickering light dulls it. Sound, temperature, posture, and even scent can alter cognitive performance. Each environmental adjustment removes one more obstacle between you and sustained thought. The goal is not aesthetic perfection, but alignment, a workspace that quietly tells your brain, "This is where work begins."

Your digital environment requires the same discipline. The modern screen is an ecosystem of distractions: notifications, tabs, open documents, unread messages, all whispering for a sliver of your focus. Every extra element is a small decision waiting to be made, and decision fatigue quickly translates into mental fatigue. Simplify your digital landscape. Keep only what directly serves your task. Mute alerts, close unused tabs, and set your devices to "Do Not Disturb" during periods of deep work. If certain platforms consume your attention habitually, make them harder to access. Move them to secondary folders, log out after use, or restrict access during focus hours. These small frictions create distance between impulse and action, giving your conscious mind time to intervene before distraction takes hold. The point is not self-denial; it is sovereignty, having ability to direct your attention where you choose, not where you are lured.

Energy is the invisible thread connecting all of this. Focus requires fuel, and when your physical or emotional reserves run low, distraction becomes irresistible. Fatigue, dehydration, poor diet, and chronic stress all weaken the circuits that govern attention. When your energy dips, your brain instinctively seeks stimulation, anything to keep itself awake. This is why you reach for your phone after long hours or scroll through social media when tired. The brain is not lazy; it is trying to stay alert by chasing novelty. To protect your focus, you must protect your energy. Sleep enough to restore cognitive control. Eat foods that provide stable energy instead of spikes and crashes. Drink water regularly. Move your body often, even briefly, to refresh circulation and reset your state. A ten-minute walk, a few stretches, or slow breathing between tasks can do more for focus than another cup of coffee. Energy and attention rise and fall together; manage one, and the other follows.

Reclaiming focus is not a one-time fix; it is a practice. The goal is not to eliminate all interruptions, but to cultivate the awareness and habits that keep them from owning you. Attention, like a muscle, strengthens with deliberate repetition. You train it by noticing when it drifts and bringing it gently back, again and again, without judgment. Each return builds resilience, each moment of presence deepens control. The process is slow but cumulative. Over weeks, you begin to feel a shift towards steadiness that replaces the constant tug of urgency. You are no longer at the mercy of noise. You choose what enters and what stays.

Here is a practical structure for applying these ideas. It serves as both a summary and a toolkit, allowing you to build your own system for focus that adapts to your life rather than dictating it.

1. **Identify your primary sources of distraction.** Spend two days observing what breaks your concentration. Note not just the external triggers, such as phone, notifications, background chatter, but the internal ones too: boredom, anxiety, fatigue. This awareness alone can reduce their power by half.
2. **Clarify your intention before each session.** Write down your main goal for the hour. Ask, "Why does this matter?" If the answer feels vague, refine it until you find meaning. Clarity naturally quiets the urge to wander because the mind prefers significance to uncertainty.
3. **Structure your time through focus intervals.**Use systems like the Pomodoro rhythm or customised time blocks that match your energy. Work in cycles of concentrated effort followed by short recovery breaks. The predictability builds trust in your own consistency.
4. **Anchor each session in a single defined action.** Start with one clear objective. One section to write, one file to edit, one concept to review. Vague goals create hesitation; concrete actions create momentum. The simpler the start, the easier the continuation.
5. **Design your physical environment for clarity and comfort.** Keep your workspace clean, well-lit, and ergonomically sound. Remove clutter, adjust temperature, and use supportive seating. Even a small act like organising your desk at the end of the day signals closure and readiness for tomorrow.

6. **Simplify your digital world.** Keep only the necessary apps and tabs open. Disable unneeded alerts. Organise your desktop and cloud folders by project to reduce visual noise. Treat your device as a workspace, not an entertainment hub.
7. **Strengthen your focus muscle daily.** Train concentration with small exercises: read for ten uninterrupted minutes, meditate on your breath, or complete a single simple task without checking your phone. Gradually increase duration. Attention grows through repetition, not intensity.
8. **Protect your energy with care.** Prioritise sleep, hydration, movement, and regular meals. Monitor your natural energy peaks and schedule demanding work during those hours. When you feel mental fatigue, take a walk or stretch rather than seeking digital stimulation.
9. **Add friction to temptation.** Make distractions slightly harder to access. Keep your phone out of arm's reach, delete shortcuts to time-wasting sites, or use focus modes on your devices. The small inconvenience gives your conscious mind time to choose differently.
10. **Review and refine weekly.** Reflect on when you focused best and when you struggled. Were you tired? Anxious? Overstimulated? Use these insights to adjust your schedule, workspace, or habits. Improvement is not found in overhaul but in ongoing refinement.

Each of these practices works because it respects the nature of the human mind. You cannot bully yourself into focus, but you can invite it by removing friction, managing energy, and clarifying purpose. Over time, the noise that once felt overwhelming begins to recede. You discover that focus, far from being an act of control, is actually an act of liberation, giving you freedom to give your best attention to what truly matters.

In the age of endless distraction, attention has become the new form of wealth. To guard it is to guard your future. Every hour reclaimed from noise is an hour given back to depth, meaning, and creation. The goal is not to manage time more tightly, but to use it more fully, to build a life where your attention is not just spent cheaply but invested wisely, one deliberate moment at a time.

ഗ്രാ

4

OVERCOMING PROCRASTINATION

Most people think procrastination is a problem of willpower, but it is really a problem of emotion. When you delay something you know you should do, it is rarely because you do not care enough. It is because some part of you associates the act of beginning with discomfort. That discomfort might be fear of failure, fear of imperfection, or fear of confronting how much effort lies ahead. Whatever its source, procrastination is a shield that protects the mind from short-term unease, even if it costs long-term peace. To understand procrastination is to understand how emotion bends time. It makes the present pain seem heavier than the future consequence, and in doing so, it teaches us to trade growth for relief.

When you hesitate before starting something meaningful, the voice inside does not say, "I don't want to do this." It says, "I don't want to feel what doing this will make me feel." The anxiety of a blank page, the dread of judgment, the fatigue of beginning after a long day. These sensations distort your sense of time. The task feels endless, even though it may only take twenty minutes. The longer you postpone, the more enormous it becomes in your imagination. This is the cruel irony of procrastination: the effort we avoid in the moment multiplies in emotional weight the longer we delay it. The clock does not move faster, but it feels as if it does, and the result is guilt layered on top of avoidance.

Fatigue intensifies this distortion. When your energy is low, tasks expand in perceived size because the brain interprets effort through the body's available resources. What could be done in half an hour at full strength can feel insurmountable after a long day of decision-making and noise. This is why the most disciplined plans often fail, not because of poor design but because they ignore physiology. You cannot outthink exhaustion. The mind obeys the body's state. To manage procrastination, you must learn to manage energy and emotion before you attempt to manage time. No strategy works on a depleted system.

At its core, procrastination is not laziness; it is avoidance of pain. Every delayed task is a negotiation between two discomforts: the discomfort of doing and the discomfort of not doing. Whichever feels greater in the moment wins. The key to overcoming procrastination is not to eliminate discomfort but to reframe it. When you interpret that tension as a signal of importance rather than danger, you begin to move differently. A difficult task becomes a sign of value, an indicator that it matters. You can then meet that discomfort with curiosity instead of resistance. This subtle shift turns avoidance into approach and transforms the emotion of fear into the energy of engagement.

The most practical way to break the cycle of delay is to shrink the scale of the beginning. The first step is almost always the hardest because it carries the full emotional weight of the task. Once you are in motion, momentum takes over and emotion recalibrates. The trick is to make the entry point so small that your brain cannot refuse it. Tell yourself you will open the file, write one line, or read one page. Do not promise yourself completion, only initiation. Once you start, inertia works in your favour. The action of beginning creates its own motivation, and the emotional resistance that felt immovable only moments before begins to dissolve. The mind is wired for progress, not perfection.

There is also a psychological law at play here called ***temporal construal***. When an event is far away in time, we think of it abstractly, with little emotional texture. As it gets closer, emotion floods the perception. That is why you can plan a project for weeks and feel fine, yet freeze the night before it is due. The emotional weight of time collapses as deadlines approach. To counter this, make the future concrete before it becomes urgent. Visualise the cost of delay not in abstract terms like "I'll regret this later," but in specific consequences: lost opportunities, broken trust, unfinished growth. The brain responds to vivid imagery, not vague warnings. When the future feels real, it gains influence over the present.

Perfectionism often hides beneath procrastination. The desire to do something flawlessly can make it impossible to begin. You delay not because you do not care, but because you care so much that the possibility of falling short feels unbearable. The solution is to separate preparation from performance. Permit yourself to create rough, imperfect drafts of your work. Treat the first version of any task as scaffolding, not structure. Once something exists, refinement becomes a matter of editing, not creation, and the emotional pressure of the blank page disappears. Progress is always more productive than paralysis.

Emotional procrastination also thrives on isolation. When you struggle alone, your fears echo louder because they meet no resistance. Sharing your goals or challenges with others, even in small ways, creates accountability and perspective. A quick conversation with a colleague, friend, or mentor can transform a mental barrier into a practical step. You realise that the task is neither as large nor as unique as you thought. Often, the act of describing what you plan to do activates the same neural circuits as beginning the task itself, priming the brain for action. Talking about work, it turns out, is sometimes the first act of doing it.

Overcoming procrastination also requires self-compassion. Harsh self-talk, the kind that says, "I'm so lazy" or "I never finish anything", only strengthens the emotional link between effort and shame. It makes starting harder, not easier. The mind resists what it associates with pain. Replace criticism with curiosity. Instead of asking, "Why can't I do this?" ask, "What am I feeling right now that makes this hard to start?" This question opens space for understanding rather than punishment. Once emotion is named, it loses much of its power to paralyse. You can address it directly, rest if you're tired, simplify if you're overwhelmed, ask for help if you're stuck.

It is also important to recognise that some delay is not avoidance but incubation. The mind often needs unstructured time to form connections beneath the surface. Not every pause is wasted time. The art lies in knowing when you are resting productively and when you are hiding. One renews you; the other erodes you. Honest reflection helps you tell the difference. When the pause begins to produce anxiety rather than insight, it is time to move. The goal is not to eliminate all delay but to make it conscious, a chosen rest rather than a passive escape.

To translate these ideas into daily life, begin with reflection. At the end of each day, ask yourself three questions:

1. What did I avoid today, and why?
2. What emotion was I trying not to feel?
3. What would have been one smaller step that I could have taken instead?

Write your answers without judgment. This exercise turns vague guilt into usable data. Patterns will emerge, such as specific times of day, particular types of tasks, predictable triggers. Once you recognise them, you can plan accordingly. Schedule difficult work for your energy peaks. Pair unappealing tasks with small rewards. Alternate between demanding and easy work to maintain balance. And most importantly, forgive yourself when you fall short. Shame adds no value to learning; curiosity does.

Ultimately, overcoming procrastination is not about becoming perfectly productive. It is about building an honest relationship over time. The more clearly you see how emotion distorts your perception of effort, the easier it becomes to move despite it. You stop waiting to feel ready and begin instead to act your way into readiness. You learn that progress is not a mood but a motion. You work steadily forward rhythm, gathering confidence as you go. When you work this way, time stops feeling like something you chase. It begins to feel like something you inhabit, fully and without fear.

ꙮ

5

THE ENERGY EQUATION

Time management often begins with calendars, lists, and plans. You block hours, set goals, and divide your day into segments of efficiency. But no schedule survives a day of fatigue. The truth is that time management without energy management is like writing plans in sand. They look impressive until the tide of exhaustion washes them away. Time gives structure to life, but energy gives it movement. Without energy, even the most precise plan collapses under its own weight.

Energy is the invisible currency that powers attention, decision-making, creativity, and emotional regulation. It determines not only how much you can do, but how well you can think, feel, and respond to the demands of the day. You have lived the difference between days when work flows effortlessly and days when every small action feels heavy. The hours are the same, but the energy behind them changes everything. Most people who feel disorganised or unmotivated are not suffering from a lack of discipline; they are suffering from energy mismanagement, trying to spend from an empty account.

Modern life drains energy in ways that are easy to overlook. Each small interruption, each minor stress, each unfinished thought consumes a portion of your internal battery. You might not notice the drain in the moment, but by midday, the cost becomes clear. Decision fatigue sets in. Attention scatters. Tasks stretch longer than they should. The brain, desperate for relief, reaches for the quickest source of stimulation, and it may be a phone, a snack, or a distraction. Anything to lift it out of depletion. The result is a paradoxical form of restlessness: you are tired yet unable to rest, overstimulated yet underfulfilled.

True productivity begins with reversing this pattern. Not by forcing yourself to push harder, but by learning to restore what effort depletes. Energy management is not about perfection or endless vitality. It is about rhythm: the deliberate alternation between effort and recovery that allows performance to remain sustainable. The body was designed to move in cycles, with peaks of concentration followed by genuine rest. When we ignore that rhythm, we invite burnout. When we honour it, time stretches; one focused hour can do the work of three distracted ones.

Physical energy is the foundation of all others. Sleep is its first law. No amount of caffeine or motivation can replace the restorative power of deep rest. During sleep, the brain clears metabolic waste, consolidates memory, and resets hormonal balance. Chronic sleep debt dulls focus, slows reaction time, and lowers emotional control, which are the very ingredients required for consistent productivity. Protecting your sleep schedule is not indulgence; it is maintenance for the system that runs every aspect of your life. If you must choose between an extra hour of work and an extra hour of rest, the latter almost always pays the greater return.

Movement, too, is a direct path to renewal. The body is designed for motion, and stagnation dulls both thought and mood. Even short bouts of physical activity recalibrate the nervous system. A brisk walk, light stretching, or brief strength training session triggers neurochemicals that heighten alertness and restore calm. You do not need long workouts; you need regular ones. Movement teaches your body to meet rising effort with stability instead of stress, to breathe through challenge instead of fleeing from it. It is both physical conditioning and cognitive training. A way to remind yourself that effort can feel alive rather than overwhelming.

Food and hydration are quieter forms of energy management but no less important. The body's fuel affects the mind's clarity. Meals that send blood sugar surging and crashing leave the brain swinging between bursts of energy and waves of lethargy. The best diet for focus is one that keeps the body steady. Indulge in regular meals that balance protein, fibre, and complex carbohydrates, paired with consistent hydration. Water intake is a simple yet powerful form of self-regulation. Even slight dehydration can reduce focus and increase irritability. Managing energy, in this sense, is not about restriction or optimisation, but about respect, and giving the body what it needs to think clearly and act deliberately.

Mental energy depends on what you allow to occupy your awareness. Each unresolved thought, each unfinished commitment, acts as an open loop in the mind. Over time, these loops consume more attention than the tasks themselves. Closing them, by deciding, delegating, or deleting, restores cognitive space. Journaling, task review, or even a simple end-of-day reflection can release mental residue that builds up through the day. The more clarity you create in thought, the less friction you feel in action.

Emotional energy is the most delicate and easily depleted form of all. It rises and falls with your sense of purpose, belonging, and inner balance. When you feel aligned with what you are doing, emotion fuels energy; when you feel disconnected or unseen, it drains it. This is why meaning is such a potent source of stamina. When effort serves a clear purpose, fatigue becomes bearable. When it does not, even small tasks feel exhausting. The surest way to renew emotional energy is to reconnect with your "why", to remind yourself what your work, your day, or your presence contributes to something larger than yourself. Gratitude also plays a role here. It reorients the mind from what is missing to what is working, from deficit to abundance. That shift is enough to restore strength.

The environment in which you work either preserves energy or leaks it. Clutter, noise, and constant connectivity all impose subtle cognitive taxes. Every object in view, every unread notification, every open tab demands micro-decisions. Simplifying your workspace is not merely about aesthetics; it is about conserving mental fuel. The fewer irrelevant details the brain must process, the more energy it can devote to what matters. Quiet surroundings, natural light, and a clear surface are not luxuries. They are environmental investments in efficiency.

To manage energy effectively, it helps to think in terms of renewal rather than depletion. Instead of asking "How much can I do today?" ask "How can I work in a way that leaves me able to do it again tomorrow?" Sustainable output comes not from intensity but from recovery. Schedule deliberate pauses between demanding tasks, such as five minutes of slow breathing, a walk, a glass of water, or a moment of stillness away from screens. Treat recovery as part of work, not an interruption to it. You do not lose time when you rest; you gain capacity when you return.

Another essential principle is alignment. Matching your most demanding work to your natural peaks of energy. Most people have one or two windows each day when alertness, focus, and creativity converge. Protect those windows from shallow work or meetings whenever possible. Use them for the projects that require depth and originality. Reserve routine or administrative tasks for lower-energy periods. This simple act of alignment often doubles productivity without extending hours.

Over time, managing energy becomes less about tactics and more about awareness. You learn to sense your internal battery, when it is full, when it is low, and what recharges it best. You begin to notice the early signs of depletion: irritability, indecision, distraction. You learn to pause before collapse rather than after. This is maturity in practice, not squeezing more from yourself, but pacing yourself wisely.

The great misunderstanding of modern productivity is that exhaustion is proof of effort. In truth, exhaustion is often proof of mismanagement. When your energy is well cared for, you can work deeply, recover quickly, and sustain performance for years without burning out. The measure of a good day is not how much you did, but how steadily you were able to give your best attention to what mattered most.

At the end of each day, ask yourself three simple questions:

1. When did my energy feel strongest, and what was I doing at that time?
2. When did it fade, and what triggered that drop?
3. What one change tomorrow would help me protect or restore that energy sooner?

These questions transform awareness into strategy. Over weeks, patterns emerge that define not only what drains you, but about what nourishes you. And once you know those patterns, you can build your time around them instead of against them.

Energy, like time, is finite within a day but renewable across days. Treat it as your most important resource. Protect it fiercely, spend it wisely, and replenish it often. The world rewards those who can stay in motion, but it is shaped by those who know how to pause, recover, and begin again with strength. Managing energy is not a soft skill; it is the hidden architecture of all sustained success.

6

THE FLOW OF FOCUS

There is a state of mind in which time seems to dissolve. The world narrows to a single task, distractions fade into silence, and every movement feels purposeful. You lose track of minutes because you are fully inside the moment. This is flow, the meeting point of challenge and capability, where effort feels almost effortless. It is not mystical, though it can feel that way. It is a psychological state triggered by clarity, difficulty, and attention. When you design your time to encourage this state, work transforms from obligation into immersion. The hours do not just pass; they expand.

Most people rarely experience deep focus anymore. Their days are filled with half-finished thoughts and constant reorientation. A message pings, a browser tab opens, a new task interrupts, and the thread of concentration breaks. Each time this happens, the brain pays a cost. Attention does not shift instantly; it lags, leaving behind what researchers call cognitive residue. When you return to the task, part of your focus remains entangled with the last thing you touched.

The mind becomes like a computer with too many programs open, just slower, hotter, and less efficient. The result is not just reduced productivity, but a subtle sense of dissatisfaction. You end the day exhausted yet strangely unfulfilled, because nothing received the depth it deserved.

Flow is the antidote to this scattered way of living. It is what happens when you give one thing your complete attention long enough for the mind to settle into its rhythm. The problem is that most environments and schedules are designed for interruption, not immersion. To experience flow consistently, you must build it deliberately. It does not arrive by accident; it arises from the conditions you create.

The first condition is clarity. The mind cannot enter deep focus on vague goals. Ambiguity scatters attention because it forces the brain to keep asking, "What exactly am I doing?" Before you begin, define the precise outcome you are working toward. The goal should be concrete enough that you know when you have reached it, but open enough to allow creativity. Instead of "work on presentation," decide, "draft the opening slide sequence." The mind relaxes when direction is clear. Clarity is the doorway to flow.

The second condition is the right level of challenge. Flow occurs when difficulty meets skill. The skill mustn't be so easy that it becomes dull, nor so hard that it triggers anxiety. Too little challenge breeds distraction; too much breeds avoidance. The ideal zone stretches your ability without snapping it. As you design your schedule, notice which tasks pull you into engagement and which push you into tension. The art is in adjusting the level of difficulty, adding structure when chaos overwhelms, and adding complexity when boredom numbs. The sweet spot between comfort and challenge is where focus comes alive.

Energy is the third condition. Flow is not a state you can force when you are depleted. Fatigue makes the mind seek shortcuts. You will reach for distractions not because you lack willpower, but because the brain, running on low fuel, is trying to preserve itself. Align your most cognitively demanding work with your natural peaks of alertness. For some, that is early morning; for others, late afternoon. The key is consistency, returning to the same window each day until your mind learns that this is the hour for depth. Over time, repetition becomes ritual, and ritual becomes readiness.

The fourth condition is environment. The physical and digital spaces you inhabit are not neutral; they either invite depth or resist it. A cluttered desk competes for attention. A phone in sight whispers for a glance. Even lighting and sound shape the mental climate. Treat your workspace as a studio for concentration. Keep what you need within reach and remove what you do not. If you work with music, choose instrumental or ambient sound that fades into the background rather than pulls you outward. If you prefer silence, create it. Close doors, wear headphones, mute notifications. Each small choice is a declaration that your attention belongs to you.

When all of these elements converge, clarity, challenge, energy, and environment, the mind begins to settle into flow. Thoughts align. Distractions fade. The passage of time shifts from something to measure to something to experience. You begin to sense continuity between effort and outcome. Work feels meaningful not because it is easy, but because it is whole. This is the difference between merely finishing tasks and inhabiting them fully.

Designing for flow is as much about what you exclude as what you include. Guard your deep work sessions as you would a meeting with someone important, because they are meetings with your own potential. Mark them on your calendar, inform others of your availability, and begin each one with a brief ritual, perhaps a few breaths, a stretch, or a review of your main goal. The mind associates ritual with readiness. When you repeat this pattern, you train yourself to slip into focus more quickly. Over time, your environment, your schedule, and your body all begin to cooperate in creating this state.

Interruptions will still happen, of course. The key is to treat them as part of the rhythm rather than as failures. If you are pulled out of flow, note the cause, resolve it if possible, and return without judgment. Attention, like a muscle, strengthens through recovery. Each time you redirect it, you deepen your capacity for future focus.

The experience of flow is deeply rewarding because it meets three of our core psychological needs: competence, autonomy, and purpose. In flow, you feel capable, in control, and connected to something meaningful. These sensations reinforce motivation far more effectively than external rewards. You no longer need to push yourself through effort; the work itself becomes its own momentum. This is why flow, once experienced regularly, becomes addictive in the best sense. It is not a craving for escape, but for engagement.

If you want to cultivate this state in your daily life, begin by simplifying your schedule. Fewer priorities mean greater depth. Block two or three hours each day for uninterrupted focus. Use the first fifteen minutes to prepare your space and clarify your target. Work with intensity for a defined period, then take a full break to reset. Protect these sessions as the sacred centre of your day. Let emails, meetings, and errands orbit around them rather than the other way around. This reversal of structure, where focus dictates the schedule instead of fitting inside it, is what separates reactive time management from intentional living.

Reflection also plays an important role. At the end of each week, review when you experienced your best focus. What conditions were present? What energy state were you in? Which environment, time of day, or type of task helped you most? Patterns will emerge. Build on them. Over time, this reflection becomes its own feedback loop, fine-tuning your approach until deep work becomes natural.

Ultimately, the flow of focus is not a luxury reserved for artists or specialists. It is a form of presence available to anyone who chooses depth over distraction. In a world that rewards speed and noise, the ability to work quietly, steadily, and completely has become a superpower. When you cultivate that ability, you stop racing against time and begin moving with it. Each hour becomes a contained universe, which leaves you feeling full, deliberate, and alive. And when your days begin to fill with hours like that, you will find that you are no longer managing time at all. You are living it.

7

WHAT TIME MANAGEMENT REALLY DOES FOR YOU

When people think of time management, they often imagine calendars, checklists, and colour-coded planners. These are useful tools, but they are not the point. The real power of managing time lies beneath the surface. It is not about squeezing more hours into a day, but about expanding the quality of the hours you already have. True time management is not the art of busyness; it is the art of presence. It is what allows you to move from living reactively to living deliberately.

Discipline is often misunderstood as restriction. People see it as a cage of schedules and obligations, something that limits freedom rather than creates it. But discipline, rightly practised, is the opposite. It is the structure that makes freedom possible. Without discipline, your time belongs to everything and everyone else. You react to messages, requests, and impulses until the day disappears in fragments. But when you take command of your time, you begin to reclaim choice.

You decide what deserves attention and what does not. You begin to experience freedom not as leisure or escape, but as the ability to direct your own energy toward what matters most.

Time management gives you this clarity. It draws a clear line between what is urgent and what is important, between what merely fills time and what fulfils it. When you live without that distinction, your days blur into a stream of activity that feels productive but leads nowhere. You go to sleep tired, yet unsatisfied, because you spent your hours reacting instead of creating. Once you learn to design your days with intention, even simple tasks begin to feel meaningful. The same hour that once slipped by unnoticed becomes a place of focus, care, and integrity.

This transformation begins subtly. As you plan your days around purpose rather than pressure, your sense of time changes. You begin to see it not as something chasing you, but as something you are shaping. The frantic edge softens. You stop racing the clock and start working with it. You discover that calm is not the absence of activity, but the presence of direction. This is one of the quiet gifts of disciplined time: it restores peace not by slowing life down, but by helping you move at your own chosen pace.

Over time, time management becomes more than a productivity system; it becomes a philosophy of living. You start noticing patterns in your energy, your emotions, and your priorities. You see where your time goes, and that awareness becomes a mirror. It shows you what you truly value. If you say family matters most, but your calendar never reflects it, the discrepancy becomes visible. If you claim you want to create, but every spare hour is spent consuming, that gap becomes undeniable. Managing time reveals the truth of your choices. It turns your schedule into a map of your beliefs.

This awareness can be uncomfortable at first because it removes the illusion that time is something happening to you. Once you see how your hours are spent, you realise that every "I didn't have time" was really an "I didn't choose to." But that discomfort is powerful. It is the moment you reclaim authorship over your life. The days no longer slip away in excuses; they begin to accumulate in meaning. You see that time is not your enemy but your canvas. Every choice, every hour, is a brushstroke in the picture you are painting of your life.

Purpose, then, is the natural outcome of disciplined time. When you act with clarity and consistency, your actions start to align with your deeper values. Work feels integrated rather than fragmented. Small habits begin to connect to larger aspirations. You begin to see how your effort today is building something lasting. That awareness replaces anxiety with quiet confidence. It gives weight to your days, not as burdens, but as contributions to a life that feels coherent.

It is also important to understand that time management is not about constant productivity. It includes knowing when to stop. Rest is not a reward for efficiency; it is part of the rhythm that sustains it. People who manage time well are not those who work endlessly, but those who know how to move between intensity and recovery without guilt. They know that true effectiveness includes restoration. They have learned that rest is not idleness; it is maintenance for the mind that creates, decides, and leads.

Another profound effect of disciplined time is that it builds trust in yourself. Each time you follow through on what you planned, you reinforce the belief that your word to yourself matters. Over weeks and months, this trust compounds into self-respect. You no longer need external motivation, because your own integrity becomes enough. This is why time management is such a powerful form of personal growth. It turns discipline into self-confidence, and self-confidence into freedom.

Eventually, the systems you build fade into the background. You no longer think in terms of planners or priorities; they become instinctive. What remains is a deeper calm, the assurance that you are living in alignment with what you value. This is the end goal of time management: not control, but harmony. You manage your hours not because you fear wasting them, but because you love what they make possible. You stop measuring success by how much you do, and start measuring it by how intentionally you live.

If you have ever watched someone truly master their time, you will notice that they seem unhurried. They move through their day with presence. They still experience challenges, interruptions, and uncertainty, but they meet them with composure. Their calm is not born of luck or simplicity; it is born of structure. They have built systems strong enough to carry them through the chaos of the day, and because of that, they can move with grace. This is what time management really does for you. It replaces panic with rhythm, distraction with depth, and survival with purpose.

Take a moment to look at your own life and ask: What is time giving me right now? Is it structure, stress, or opportunity? How does my calendar reflect my values? What would it look like to shape my time so that it reflects not just what I need to do, but who I want to become? These questions are not logistical; they are existential. They mark the shift from managing minutes to managing meaning.

When you live this way, discipline no longer feels like a sacrifice. It feels like strength. You understand that structure does not confine you but supports you. You begin to see that time is not something to master, but something to be in relationship with. And that relationship, like any meaningful one, requires care, attention, and respect. When you give those to your hours, they return them to your life tenfold.

Time management, at its highest form, is self-mastery expressed through rhythm. It teaches you that freedom is not the absence of responsibility, but the ability to act on purpose. When you live with that understanding, every hour has potential. Every choice becomes a declaration of what matters. And every day, no matter how ordinary, becomes a deliberate act of becoming who you are meant to be.

ꟸ

8

TIME AS A LIFESTYLE

Time management is not simply a collection of techniques to squeeze more tasks into fewer hours. At its highest form, it is a philosophy of living. It is the practice of shaping your days in a way that honours your values and sustains your energy over the long term. The aim is not to dominate time but to live in rhythm with it, to build a life that feels coherent and grounded instead of rushed and fragmented. When time management becomes a lifestyle, it stops being about productivity alone. It becomes about fulfilment, about creating a steady pace that allows you to grow, contribute, and rest without losing your sense of direction.

Living with rhythm requires you to see time not as a resource to be consumed, but as an ecosystem to be cared for. Just as a natural environment needs periods of daylight and darkness, activity and stillness, your life requires balance between effort and recovery. Modern culture often glorifies constant motion, the endless push toward achievement, but time has its own logic. Without renewal, performance collapses. Without pauses, even the most meaningful work loses texture. To live with time instead of against it, you must learn to move between intensity and ease with awareness. That balance is not a luxury; it is a prerequisite for lasting success.

Many people chase efficiency without realising that what they truly crave is peace. They fill their schedules with meetings, errands, and goals, believing that busyness equals importance. Yet what often follows is depletion, an erosion of joy, creativity, and clarity. The myth of busyness hides a deeper truth: we are not designed to operate in perpetual urgency. The human mind, like the body, functions best in cycles of expansion and recovery. Recognising this and building your life around it changes everything. When you begin to respect your natural cadence, you no longer fight against time. You begin to flow with it.

Creating that flow starts with designing a daily rhythm that reflects both your responsibilities and your humanity. Every person's rhythm is different, shaped by personality, energy patterns, and the nature of their work. The goal is not to replicate someone else's schedule but to find the pace that keeps you both productive and well. For many people, this means identifying three kinds of time: focus time, maintenance time, and renewal time. Focus time is when you dedicate yourself fully to meaningful work, free from distractions. Maintenance time includes the necessary but routine tasks that keep your life running smoothly. Renewal time is for rest, reflection, and recreation. It is the space where your mind and body repair themselves. Balancing these three forms of time creates a sustainable rhythm for living and working well.

To bring this balance into practice, begin by mapping your week. Write down your major tasks and responsibilities, then assign them to categories of focus, maintenance, or renewal. You might find that focus time gets all your attention while renewal barely appears, or that maintenance tasks have quietly expanded to fill your schedule. Awareness is the first act of change. Once you see how your time is distributed, adjust intentionally. Protect your focus hours for meaningful work, schedule your maintenance tasks efficiently, and honour renewal as a non-negotiable priority. Renewal is not indulgence. The body and mind are tools; they cannot perform well if never allowed to recover.

Rest is one of the most undervalued aspects of time management. It is not the absence of activity; it is an active form of repair. The brain consolidates learning, creativity, and emotional balance during rest. Yet many people treat it as a reward for productivity rather than a requirement for it. If you constantly postpone rest until you are exhausted, you teach your mind that recovery is optional, which eventually leads to burnout. A healthier approach is to integrate small, deliberate moments of stillness into your day, a short walk after lunch, a few minutes of slow breathing between meetings, a quiet evening routine that signals closure. These moments act like punctuation marks in the narrative of your day, turning chaos into cadence.

Fulfilment also depends on renewal at a deeper level, which is emotional and spiritual renewal. This can mean spending time in nature, nurturing relationships, engaging in a creative hobby, or simply allowing yourself to think without an agenda. These activities may not appear “productive” in a conventional sense, but they renew the emotional reserves that sustain focus and motivation. Without them, even the best time management systems become mechanical. Your life becomes a series of completed tasks rather than a meaningful journey. Renewal reminds you that the purpose of managing time is to make space for what makes life worth living.

To apply this philosophy practically, consider this reflection framework:

1. **Audit your time.** For one week, track how much time you spend in focus, maintenance, and renewal. Observe the imbalance without judgment.
2. **Redefine productivity.** Identify which activities replenish you rather than merely occupy you. Productivity includes the ability to restore your energy, not just expend it.
3. **Establish closing rituals.** End your day with a small act that separates work from life, writing a short reflection, tidying your desk, or stepping outside for fresh air. These signals help your mind reset.
4. **Protect your margins.** Leave unscheduled spaces between commitments. These open moments allow for reflection and recovery, and often become the birthplace of your best ideas.
5. **Renew regularly.** Schedule rest as seriously as work. Whether it's an afternoon of reading, a weekly digital break, or a yearly retreat, deliberate pauses prevent emotional exhaustion.

These practices gradually turn time management into a lifestyle, one that values rhythm over rush and renewal over repetition. When you live this way, you begin to experience time differently. Hours no longer feel like units to fill but moments to inhabit fully. You become less reactive, more intentional, and more at peace with the natural pace of your life.

Living with time also means embracing imperfection. No rhythm stays perfect. Some days will overflow with effort; others will drift. The point is not to control every moment but to return to alignment when you lose it. This is what makes time management sustainable. It is not the unbroken execution of a plan but the ongoing act of rebalancing. You learn to sense when you are pushing too hard or slipping too far, and you make gentle corrections instead of harsh judgments. In doing so, you build a relationship with time that is grounded in awareness rather than anxiety.

Time as a lifestyle is about presence. It is about bringing your full attention to whatever moment you are in, whether it is work, rest, or connection. When you cultivate this awareness, even ordinary hours feel rich. You begin to live days that are not just filled but felt with structure and space, both ambition and ease. Over time, this balance becomes your default state. You stop measuring your worth by output and begin measuring it by harmony.

In the end, the purpose of mastering time is not to achieve more but to live better. You are not here to race the clock; you are here to understand it, to move with it, and to fill it with meaning. The rhythm you create today becomes the melody of your life. Treat it with care, with patience, and with grace.

9

PERSONALISING PRODUCTIVITY

Every person is different, yet so many people approach productivity as if there were a single formula that fits everyone. They try to copy systems that worked for someone else, taking a morning routine from a book, a planner layout from a colleague, a rigid schedule from a podcast, and then wonder why it collapses after a few days. The truth is simple but often overlooked: productivity cannot be borrowed. It has to be built. The systems that truly work are not the most efficient or most popular, but the ones that are honest reflections of who you are, how you think, and what you value. The moment you stop forcing yourself into someone else's rhythm and begin to understand your own, your effort becomes lighter and your results become stronger.

Human beings are complex organisms, not machines that can run the same way each day. We are guided by temperament, biology, emotion, and circumstance. A person who draws energy from interaction will not thrive under long hours of solitude, just as someone who finds meaning in quiet focus will feel constantly drained in noisy, reactive environments. Understanding this is the foundation of personal productivity. It means looking inward before looking outward, studying how you naturally function, and creating systems that support that reality. When your structure matches your nature, you no longer feel as though discipline is a fight. It becomes a form of cooperation between your goals and your inner rhythm.

Temperament plays a defining role in this alignment. Some people crave order and predictability; they find clarity in routine and comfort in planning. Others feel most alive when they are responding to inspiration rather than following a plan. Some enjoy collaboration, feeding off collective energy and shared accountability, while others find their best ideas in solitude. Instead of labelling these differences as strengths or weaknesses, see them as instructions. The person who loves structure should embrace it unapologetically. The person who thrives on flexibility should allow for fluidity in their schedule, trusting that creativity often appears in open space. Productivity begins not when you conquer your tendencies, but when you learn to work with them intelligently.

You can begin understanding your temperament by quietly observing your daily patterns. Notice how you start your morning and how your energy shifts as the day progresses. Do you feel most alert before sunrise or after sunset? Do you concentrate best in silence or with background sound? Do you find yourself recharged after social interaction or after time alone? Record these small discoveries for a week or two. They will reveal more about how you work than any motivational framework ever could. Once you recognise your natural preferences, design your workflow accordingly. If you are an early riser, schedule deep, creative work at dawn and reserve afternoons for lighter tasks. If your focus strengthens at night, shape your day so that your mornings include simpler or administrative work, leaving your best mental energy for when it naturally arrives.

Energy cycles are another layer of self-understanding. Everyone experiences rises and dips in focus, motivation, and physical vitality. Ignoring these cycles leads to burnout; working with them leads to flow. Most people try to push through low-energy periods, mistaking exhaustion for laziness. In reality, fatigue is data. It signals the need for restoration or redirection.

Pay attention to your body's language. When concentration slips, step away for a moment. When your thoughts become sluggish, move, stretch, or walk. Notice what habits refill your energy and which ones drain it. Over time, you will develop a map of your natural peaks and valleys, which allows you to plan your day intelligently. This is not indulgence; it is strategy. You do not lose time by resting at the right moments. You gain clarity and endurance for the hours that matter most.

Energy cycles also operate on larger scales. Weeks, months, and even seasons carry their own patterns of expansion and contraction. For instance, some people feel highly creative and driven during certain months, while others experience quieter, reflective periods. There are also life seasons to consider. The system that worked for you as a student may not serve you as a parent, a leader, or an entrepreneur. Each role brings new rhythms and new limitations. Productivity that refuses to adapt to your current reality becomes a form of resistance. Growth requires adjustment. Learning to modify your systems as your life evolves is an act of wisdom, not weakness. You are allowed to change how you operate without losing your discipline.

A personalised system begins with awareness but deepens through design. Once you understand your patterns, start translating them into structure. Think of yourself as a designer building a workflow that feels natural to inhabit. Begin by identifying three elements: your focus hours, your recharge practices, and your maintenance habits. Focus hours are when your attention is sharpest and your output strongest. Protect these fiercely. Make them distraction-free and reserve them for your most meaningful work. Recharge practices are the activities that help you recover energy, such as reading, walking, or spending time in conversation. Maintenance habits are the small routines that keep your system running, such as reviewing plans, organising materials, or clearing your workspace. When these three elements are in balance, you create a sustainable rhythm of effort, renewal, and recalibration.

To help guide your experimentation, use this expanded framework:

Understand your temperament. Notice your natural tendencies without judgment. Are you structured or spontaneous, social or solitary, analytical or intuitive? Build routines that express those qualities rather than suppress them.

Identify your energy cycles. Track when your focus and motivation are at their highest. Align demanding work with your peaks and lighter activities with your dips. This is how you multiply your effectiveness without extending your hours.

Adapt to your season of life. Accept that every chapter requires new methods. A young professional's rhythm may not suit a parent of two or someone managing a team. Redesign your systems to reflect your current responsibilities, not a past version of yourself.

Experiment with structure. Try different approaches: time blocking, themed days, task batching, or momentum chaining (where small wins build into larger effort). Observe which patterns feel natural. Keep what works, release what does not.

Review regularly. Set aside quiet moments every few weeks to reflect. Ask yourself what feels easy and what feels forced. Make small corrections before the imbalance becomes fatigue, and remember: productivity is not about perfection, it is about ongoing refinement.

This framework is not a checklist; it is a living process. The more you practice it, the more attuned you become to your own rhythms. Over time, your system will start to feel less like a tool and more like a companion, as something that grows with you. You will begin to recognise that productivity is not about effort alone, but about alignment. The right system makes discipline feel less like a struggle and more like a natural state.

It is also important to resist the illusion that optimisation is endless. Many people become trapped in constant tinkering, endlessly tweaking their planners, apps, and colour codes while avoiding the work itself. Personalisation is not about decoration. It is about clarity. A functional system simplifies your day, not complicates it. It gives you more time to live, not more to manage. When your methods become an obstacle, strip them back to their essence: what helps you start, stay focused, and finish? Keep only that.

The deeper reward of personalisation is self-trust. Once you understand how you function, you no longer depend on external motivation to begin. You no longer need to copy someone else's morning ritual or chase the latest technique. You can rely on your own rhythm. That confidence becomes self-perpetuating. You design your days with awareness, follow through with ease, and recover without guilt. Your productivity becomes not a borrowed system but a reflection of self-knowledge.

Ultimately, personal productivity is not a mechanical formula. It is a practice of self-respect. It is the art of listening to your own signals and building a structure that honours them. When you work in harmony with your temperament, your cycles, and your season of life, time becomes a partner rather than a pressure. You stop measuring success by how many boxes you tick and begin to measure it by how whole you feel at the end of the day. This is the shift from imitation to authenticity, from exhaustion to flow. Once you reach that point, productivity stops being something you chase and becomes something you live.

ΣΟϹΖ

10

CREATING LASTING CHANGE

Lasting change rarely happens in a single burst of motivation. It takes root through rhythm and repetition. You do not transform your life by doing something once; you transform it by doing it consistently until it becomes part of who you are. The challenge is not to build a plan but to keep it alive long enough for it to take hold. Most people begin strong but fade because they mistake excitement for discipline. They design elaborate systems, download the latest tools, and feel a surge of clarity. But when the novelty wears off, so does their effort. The real work begins after enthusiasm fades. That is the moment when structure must turn into habit and habit into identity.

Habits are not rigid routines. They are quiet agreements you make with yourself about how you will spend your time and energy. A habit that lasts does not rely on perfection; it relies on design. When you remove friction, add clarity, and connect each habit to something meaningful, consistency becomes natural. A well-formed habit feels less like forcing yourself to act and more like following the path of least resistance. You do not have to push yourself to brush your teeth or tie your shoes each morning because the behaviour has been repeated enough to become automatic. The same principle applies to meaningful change. When you practice a behaviour in stable conditions and reward it through progress or satisfaction, it becomes self-sustaining.

Think of lasting change as a process with three layers: structure, habit, and identity. Structure is the external framework. It works as the systems and schedules that support your goals. Habit is the repetition that stabilises those systems over time, and identity is the final integration, when you no longer act out of obligation but out of alignment with who you believe yourself to be. For instance, someone who says, "I am trying to exercise," still sees fitness as something external. But the person who says, "I am an active person," has moved beyond effort into identity. Once you see yourself as the kind of person who does something, you no longer need to negotiate with yourself about doing it. The decision is made at the level of identity, not willpower.

A simple but powerful example of this is morning routines. Many people struggle to wake up early and begin their day with focus. At first, it feels like a daily battle between comfort and intention. But when the act of waking early becomes linked to identity: "I am someone who begins my day with purpose", the habit stabilises. Over time, the identity becomes self-reinforcing. You begin to prepare for the morning by sleeping earlier, keeping your space organised, or setting aside clothes and tasks in advance. Each small action confirms the belief and strengthens the system. The same pattern applies to reading regularly, exercising, journaling, or any practice that shapes the person you want to become.

To create habits that last, you need both design and reflection. The design is external: it focuses on reducing resistance and supporting repetition. The reflection is internal: it focuses on understanding why the habit matters and how it aligns with your values. Here is a practical way to approach both dimensions.

1. **Start small, stay steady.** Choose a habit so small that failure is nearly impossible. If you want to begin exercising, commit to five minutes a day. If you want to read more, start with one page. If you want to organise your day, begin by writing down one priority. Consistency, not scale, creates the foundation. Once a small habit stabilises, expansion is easy. The mind resists big changes but embraces small ones when repeated reliably.
2. **Design your environment.** Make the habit obvious and accessible. If you want to write daily, keep your notebook open on your desk. If you want to eat better, place healthier options at eye level. If you want to stretch every morning, leave a mat where you can see it. Environments either reinforce or resist your intentions. When your surroundings support your goals, willpower becomes almost unnecessary.
3. **Connect the habit to a trigger.** Habits are strongest when linked to a consistent cue. Tie your new habit to an existing behaviour. For example, after brushing your teeth, meditate for two minutes; after turning on your laptop, review your top three tasks. These anchors reduce the need for decision-making, allowing habits to blend naturally into your day.
4. **Reward progress.** The brain learns through reward. Celebrate small wins, whether a completed session, a streak, or a visible improvement. You do not need grand rewards; acknowledgement

is enough. A simple checkmark in a journal or a quiet "well done" to yourself helps encode satisfaction and reinforces the habit loop. Over time, the reward shifts from external markers to the intrinsic pleasure of the act itself.

5. **Reflect regularly.** Every few weeks, step back and assess. Ask what is working and what feels forced. Are you still aligned with your purpose? Has the habit become a burden, or does it still serve growth? Reflection prevents rigidity. It allows you to adapt without abandoning your progress.
6. **Link habits to identity.** This is the ultimate step. Write a sentence that begins with "I am the kind of person who…" and finish it with the quality you want to embody. Revisit that sentence often. The goal is not to force behaviour but to cultivate self-perception. When identity takes root, consistency follows naturally.

Creating lasting change also requires patience. Many people abandon habits too soon because they expect transformation to feel dramatic. In truth, change often feels ordinary. You may not notice progress until you look back weeks later and realise that something that once required effort now happens automatically. That quiet normalisation is the real signal of growth. Just as a seed grows beneath the soil long before it breaks the surface, your efforts take time to become visible. Trust the process and remain steady.

The science of habit formation supports this. Studies on behavioural psychology show that repetition in stable conditions creates neural pathways that make actions automatic. Each time you repeat a behaviour, the brain strengthens the connection, reducing the effort required to initiate it next time. Consistency is the fertiliser of change. When effort becomes ritual, identity begins to form around it.

Consider a professional who once struggled with disorganisation. Every morning was a rush; misplaced documents, missed emails, and half-finished plans. Frustration led to exhaustion. Then she decided to change one thing: every evening before leaving her desk, she would take five minutes to organise her workspace and list her top priorities for the next day. At first, it felt trivial. But after a few weeks, mornings became smoother. Her mind felt clearer. Eventually, she stopped seeing it as a task and began to see herself as a prepared person. That small shift in identity: "I am someone who plans", changed her performance, confidence, and calm. One habit rewrote the tone of her days.

Lasting change is not about doing more; it is about becoming more consistent with what matters most. When your habits are aligned with your values, they create stability even when life is unpredictable. The person who builds habits around mindfulness, exercise, gratitude, or organisation carries a quiet strength into every challenge. Discipline is no longer about effort. It becomes a reflection of identity.

In the end, the goal of structure and routine is not to limit you but to free you. Good habits create space, space for creativity, reflection, and joy. They remove the chaos that drains your attention and replace it with calm predictability. Over time, this consistency compounds into character. The things you once struggled to do become part of how you live, and that steadiness begins to shape every area of your life.

The beauty of habit is that it does not demand perfection, only presence. When you miss a day, you return the next. When you fall, you rebuild. The strength of habit is not in never breaking but in always returning. The habit becomes the anchor that steadies you through distraction, fatigue, and uncertainty. Once your structure becomes a habit and your habit becomes identity, lasting change no longer depends on willpower. It simply becomes who you are.

ꕤ

11

THE TIMELESS MINDSET

The highest form of time management is not about getting more done. It is about changing your relationship with time itself. The timeless mindset invites you to step away from the race to fit everything into a day and instead learn how to experience the day fully. It replaces control with cooperation, rush with rhythm, and anxiety with awareness. You stop treating time as a scarce resource that is always slipping away and begin to see it as a partner in creating meaning. To live this way is to realise that time does not have to be managed like a machine. It has to be understood, respected, and lived with attention.

Modern life teaches us to value speed above all else. We are told to move fast, to multitask, to always be producing something visible. The constant motion feels productive, yet beneath the surface, it often leads to exhaustion and dissatisfaction. You finish the day with a long list of completed tasks and an empty feeling that nothing truly important was touched. The faster you move, the less you notice. The timeless mindset begins by questioning this assumption that speed equals success. The truth is that most of what gives life depth and meaning unfolds slowly. Growth, mastery, healing, and creativity require sustained presence. They are built not in moments of rush but in moments of quiet persistence.

Presence is the foundation of this new way of seeing time. Most people live caught between two invisible forces: regret about what has passed and anxiety about what might come. Their attention is split, their energy scattered, and their days feel shorter because they are rarely fully inside them. The mind becomes a time traveller, constantly jumping ahead or backwards, rarely landing in the moment where life actually happens. Presence is the act of calling your mind home to the now. It means noticing what is in front of you without judgment or distraction. When you are present, even ordinary tasks take on richness. You begin to taste your food, hear your surroundings, and sense the rhythm of your own breathing. Work becomes less about completion and more about participation.

Cultivating presence is a practice, not a switch. It starts with awareness of your own pace. Imagine you are writing an email. Halfway through, your phone buzzes, a notification lights up, and your attention fractures. You respond out of reflex, then return to the email only to find your focus dulled. The task now feels heavier than before. This tiny moment reveals how much attention costs. Try instead to pause, breathe, and gently bring your focus back. If you do this enough times, you begin to train your brain to hold attention without constant flight. Presence strengthens the more you practice returning to it. Like a muscle, it becomes reliable through repetition.

Patience grows from this presence. When you are fully engaged in the process, you stop demanding that every effort immediately pay off. You understand that meaningful outcomes mature with time. Think of a gardener planting seeds. The soil looks the same day after day, yet underground, life is forming. The gardener does not dig up the seeds to check their progress. They water, protect, and trust the process. The same principle applies to personal growth. Whether you are learning a language, building a business, or developing a new habit, the results are invisible for a while. The impatient person abandons the effort, convinced nothing is happening. The patient person continues, confident that persistence itself is progress. This patience transforms frustration into peace.

Consider the example of a musician practising the same passage of a song for hours. At first, it feels clumsy and repetitive. But somewhere between the fiftieth and the hundredth repetition, something changes. The motion becomes natural, the rhythm easier. What once required conscious thought now flows effortlessly. This is the reward of patience, the quiet turning of time into skill. The same can be said for writers who draft pages that will never be published, athletes who train in silence before they compete, or parents who guide their children through endless small lessons that bloom only years later. The timeless mindset teaches that nothing worthwhile is wasted when approached with patience and attention.

Another essential aspect of this mindset is finding your pace. Time has texture. It moves differently for each person and each task. Some hours are best for intense focus, others for quiet reflection, and others for rest. Many people live out of sync with their natural rhythm, forcing themselves to work against their energy. They treat every hour as equal and wonder why motivation fades. The truth is, rhythm matters more than schedule. Observe when your mind feels sharpest, when you feel most creative, and when fatigue sets in. Then design your day around that flow. For instance, if your clearest thinking happens early, reserve those hours for deep work and leave routine tasks for later. If creativity sparks in the evening, allow that space to remain open rather than filling it with distractions.

You can deepen this awareness through what might be called rhythm mapping. For one week, record how you feel at different times of the day. Rate your energy and focus from one to ten. Then look for patterns. You may discover that your energy peaks mid-morning or that you feel mentally slow after lunch. Once you see the rhythm, you can align your work with it instead of fighting against it. A writer might choose to draft in the morning, edit in the afternoon, and plan in the evening. A student might study complex subjects in their most alert hours and reserve lighter work for later. Living with your natural pace is not indulgent; it is intelligent. It ensures that effort flows where it will be most effective.

This mindset also changes how you view failure. In traditional time management, failure feels like a delay, an interruption to progress. In the timeless mindset, failure is seen as part of the rhythm. Every mistake contains information that helps refine your process. Think of an artist sketching a portrait. The first lines are rarely perfect. They guide the hand, reveal proportion, and prepare the eye to see better. Each imperfect sketch makes the next one stronger. In the same way, every misstep in life, every project that does not unfold as planned, teaches you something about timing, method, or patience. When you stop fearing failure as wasted time, you learn to use it as feedback. The time spent learning is never lost.

Reflection is another key to sustaining the timeless mindset. It transforms experience into understanding. At the end of the day, take a few quiet minutes to review what truly mattered. Ask yourself: where was I most present today? When did I feel most scattered? What moments felt longer because I was absorbed in them? Reflection helps you see how your attention shapes your perception of time. Notice that the moments when you were fully engaged, like a meaningful conversation, a creative flow, a walk outdoors, often felt expansive, while distracted moments vanished without a trace. Presence stretches time; distraction shrinks it. Once you understand this, you naturally begin to live more intentionally.

The timeless mindset is not only for personal peace. It is also practical. When you live with presence, patience, and pace, you make better decisions. You stop reacting to urgency and begin responding with clarity. You prioritise work that aligns with your values, because you are no longer seduced by the illusion of constant busyness. You give your best energy to what matters and let the rest pass without guilt. Over time, this approach does not just improve your productivity but also changes your quality of life. You feel less hurried, yet you accomplish more. You feel calmer, yet more focused. You find that time, once your opponent, has become your ally.

The shift is subtle but profound. Imagine two people walking through the same park. One is rushing to finish a phone call, thinking about emails and deadlines. The other notices the light filtering through the trees, the rhythm of their steps, the sound of the wind. They occupy the same physical space, but their experience of time is entirely different. The first moves through minutes; the second moves through moments. The timeless mindset trains you to live like the second person; aware, grounded, and alive in each step.

To live this way requires trust: trust that slowing down will not make you fall behind, trust that patience will lead to deeper rewards, and trust that presence is enough. In the beginning, this can feel uncomfortable because it contradicts what society rewards. Yet those who practice it find something extraordinary. Their days begin to feel whole. They stop rushing through life and start inhabiting it. Their work becomes richer, their relationships more meaningful, and their sense of time expands.

Ultimately, the timeless mindset is not about managing the hours of your day but about mastering the experience of your life. It teaches you to balance effort with ease, to allow time to unfold without resistance, and to bring full awareness to whatever you are doing. When you live this way, time no longer feels like something slipping away. It feels like something you are a part of, flowing, steady, and alive. You stop trying to outrun it and instead learn to move with it. That is the real mastery of time: not control, but harmony.

ജ്ഞ

CONCLUSION

The Art of Living in Time

Time cannot be owned, saved, or controlled. It moves forward, silently and without pause, carrying every one of us along in its current. Yet within that current lies a choice that defines how we live: we can either fight against time, struggling to master it, or we can learn to move with it, understanding its rhythm and allowing it to guide us toward meaning. The purpose of this book has never been to teach control but to teach harmony. True time management is not about conquering hours; it is about learning how to inhabit them fully.

Every tool and method you have encountered so far, goal setting, prioritisation, focus, and reflection, has served one greater purpose: to help you reclaim awareness. Awareness turns time from an invisible background into a living companion. Without it, the days blur into one another, and even accomplishment begins to feel hollow. People often believe they are managing time when they are really just filling it. The calendar is packed, the checklist is long, the inbox is cleared, and yet a quiet unease remains. The problem is not a lack of organisation; it is a lack of connection. A full schedule without a clear sense of purpose becomes noise, and in that noise, presence disappears.

To live well within time, you must return to presence. This begins when you notice how easily your attention is scattered, how the mind drifts to what was or what might be, rarely resting in what is. You spend hours worrying about the future or replaying the past, while the present moment waits quietly to be lived. Presence asks that you bring your whole self to this moment, whatever it contains. It does not demand perfection, only sincerity. It is the awareness that even this very breath, this small action, this conversation, holds the essence of life. When you give your full attention to it, time slows down. The hour stretches and deepens because you are finally inside it.

This awareness transforms even ordinary routines. Drinking your morning coffee, answering emails, or walking to work are no longer intervals between the "real" parts of life. They become life itself. When you bring mindfulness to each act, you stop measuring time by speed or quantity and begin to measure it by quality. You begin to understand that the difference between a rushed day and a meaningful one is not in what happens but in how awake you are for it.

Living in time rather than against it also requires patience. Modern life has trained us to crave immediacy. We expect quick answers, instant responses, and rapid results. Yet the most important things we build, such as trust, mastery, love, and character, require long, steady investment. Patience is not the absence of ambition but the presence of depth. It is the courage to continue even when progress feels invisible. A student who studies daily without yet understanding the full picture, an artist layering colour over weeks before the image takes form, or a leader guiding a team through uncertainty, all are practising patience. Time, when met with consistent effort and trust, transforms intention into achievement.

Patience also means releasing the need for constant acceleration. The culture of speed often convinces us that rest is weakness and stillness is waste. Yet nature itself teaches the opposite. The seasons change at their own pace; the seed does not rush to become a tree. Every form of life unfolds according to its rhythm. When you align your life with this natural rhythm, you begin to find strength in balance. There are moments meant for focused work and others meant for rest. The mind, like the body, performs best when it breathes. Without pauses, you lose perspective; without rhythm, you lose sustainability. Learning to alternate between motion and renewal is not inefficiency; it is wisdom.

Reflection is what gives this wisdom direction. At the end of a day, or even a week, take a few quiet minutes to look back. Ask yourself what truly mattered, what felt meaningful, and what drained you. These small reflections act like a compass, guiding you toward alignment between your time and your values. Over weeks and months, reflection builds self-knowledge. You begin to see patterns: what energises you, what wastes your time, what brings peace. This understanding allows you to design your days more intentionally, not out of rigid control but out of clear purpose.

Gratitude deepens this practice. It is not merely the act of saying "thank you" for the good things that happen. Gratitude is a shift in perception. It reminds you that this moment, as it is, already contains something worth appreciating. Gratitude slows the pace of life by anchoring you in what is present rather than what is missing. When you pause to acknowledge what is already working, you stop rushing through your days as if fulfilment lies somewhere ahead. You realise it is already here, in the quiet beauty of ordinary time.

Acceptance is another part of the art of living in time. You cannot control every outcome or anticipate every turn. Plans will change, setbacks will arrive, and sometimes the hours will feel heavier than they should. The timeless mindset teaches that resistance multiplies stress, while acceptance opens the path to clarity. Acceptance does not mean passivity. It means recognising reality as it is, and then responding with wisdom rather than panic. When you accept the present fully, you waste less time wishing for another version of it. You conserve energy for action and recover faster from disruption. Acceptance is not surrender; it is intelligent cooperation with time.

Think of the difference between two people facing the same storm. One stands rigid, fighting the wind, frustrated by what they cannot change. The other adjusts their sail, letting the wind guide their direction. Both encounter the same force of nature, but only one moves forward. Time, like wind, cannot be stopped or slowed. It can only be understood and navigated. The art lies in adjusting your sail.

This way of living changes how you experience success. In a world obsessed with measurement, hours worked, deadlines met, and goals achieved, it takes courage to value depth over volume. Yet true success is not how much you accomplish in a lifetime but how deeply you inhabit your days. You can live a long life without ever being fully present, or you can live fewer years with such awareness that every moment feels full. The timeless mindset invites you to trade quantity for quality, speed for depth, and urgency for intention.

To live like this requires a new kind of discipline. Not the discipline of pushing harder, but the discipline of staying aware. It takes effort to keep returning to the present when distraction is constant. It takes maturity to choose patience when results are slow. It takes strength to rest when the world glorifies exhaustion. Yet these choices are the essence of mastery. Each time you pause to breathe, each time you choose presence over haste, you reclaim a small piece of your life from chaos.

The final lesson of time management is simple: no one truly manages time. We manage attention. We decide where to place it, how long to keep it there, and what meaning to create through it. The hours will pass whether you fill them or not. What matters is the quality of awareness you bring to them. When your attention is aligned with your values, time becomes an ally. When it is scattered, time becomes a thief. The power lies not in the clock, but in your consciousness.

The art of living in time is the art of being fully awake to life. It asks you to slow down, to look around, and to participate deeply in your own existence. It asks you to create space between moments instead of rushing through them. It teaches you that efficiency without presence is emptiness and that productivity without peace is just motion. To live well in time is to find meaning in both doing and being, to work when it is time to work and to rest when it is time to rest, to move forward and to pause.

When you begin to live this way, you stop feeling like you are chasing life. You begin to feel like you are part of it. The ticking clock no longer sounds like a warning; it sounds like a rhythm. Every moment, no matter how small, becomes an opportunity to create, to feel, to love, and to grow. You no longer ask, "How much time do I have left?" but "How deeply can I live the time I have?" That is the real art of time, not to manage it, but to experience it.

ജ്ര

THE TIME MASTERY TOOLKIT

A Practical Framework for Living Intentionally in Time

This toolkit brings together the key methods, mindsets, and daily actions introduced throughout the book. Use it not as a rigid checklist, but as a living guide, something you return to often, adjusting as your life and priorities evolve. The goal is not perfection. The goal is alignment: to live with time instead of chasing it.

1. **The Foundation: Awareness and Intention**

   Before you plan your time, learn to *see* your time. Awareness of your time creates the clarity needed for meaningful change.

Daily Practice:

- Begin each morning by asking: *What truly matters today?*
- Identify your top 3 priorities, not just tasks, but outcomes that align with your values.
- Observe how you spend your hours currently. Notice what drains you, what restores you, what forwards your goals, and what simply fills space.
- End your day with a five-minute reflection: *Where was I most present? Where did I drift? What will I do differently tomorrow?*

Reminders:

- Awareness is not judgment. You are learning how time feels, not grading your performance.
- Intention starts small. Even one mindful hour changes the tone of a day.

2. **Goal Setting and Prioritisation System**

Step 1: Define Your Goals Using the SMART Method

- **Specific:** What exactly do I want to achieve?
- **Measurable:** How will I know I've succeeded?
- **Achievable:** Is this realistic with my current resources?
- **Relevant:** Does this goal reflect what matters most to me?
- **Time-Bound:** When will I take action or complete this?

Step 2: Apply the Eisenhower Matrix Use this matrix to separate urgency from importance.

- **Quadrant I:** Urgent & Important → Do now.
- **Quadrant II:** Important but Not Urgent → Schedule and protect time for these.
- **Quadrant III:** Urgent but Not Important → Delegate or minimise.
- **Quadrant IV:** Neither Urgent nor Important → Eliminate or limit.

Step 3: The 80/20 Principle

- Identify the 20% of tasks that produce 80% of your results.
- Focus on deep work that creates long-term value, not short-term noise.

Weekly Reset Prompt:

- What single action this week will create the biggest positive ripple across my goals?

3. **The Planning Framework**

Daily Structure Template

Time Block	Task or Theme	Focus Level	Notes
Morning (High Energy)	Deep Work or Creative Tasks	8–10/10	Protect this block. No distractions.
Midday	Meetings, Collaboration, Calls	6–7/10	Batch similar activities.
Afternoon	Admin, Email, Routine Work	5–6/10	Keep tasks light and contained.
Evening	Reflection, Learning, Wind Down	3–4/10	Disconnect and restore.

Tips for Effective Planning:

- Use both analogue (notebooks, journals) and digital tools (calendars, reminders) to build a system that suits your habits.
- Review your planner every morning and evening.
- Plan your next day before you finish the current one.
- Colour-code your categories: Focus, Family, Health, Learning, Rest.

Weekly Planning Ritual:

- Every Sunday or Monday morning, review your previous week.
- Note your three key wins, three challenges, and one improvement for next week.
- Schedule what matters most before anything else.

4. **Energy and Focus Management**

Daily Energy Check: Rate your physical, mental, and emotional energy from 1–10.

- Below 5 → Rest, hydrate, move your body, step outside.
- 6–8 → Moderate tasks and collaborative work.
- 9–10 → Deep focus and creative or strategic work.

Focus Strategies:

- Try the **Pomodoro Rhythm**: 25 minutes focus + 5 minutes rest. After 4 sessions, take a 20-minute break.
- Practice single-tasking: One focus, one window, one intention.
- Eliminate multitasking: It divides attention and multiplies fatigue.
- Create a "Distraction Audit." List your top 5 habitual distractions and plan how you will limit each.

Environmental Support:

- Keep your workspace clear, well-lit, and comfortable.
- Adjust your space before you begin, not during your work.
- Use cues to trigger focus: a specific chair, a scent, or a background sound.

Reflection Prompts:

- What part of the day felt most productive?
- What triggered the distraction?
- How often did I feel present and engaged?
- What can I change tomorrow to feel more aligned?

Weekly Review Questions:

- What did I achieve that truly mattered?
- What did I postpone, and why?
- What can I simplify or eliminate?
- What moments felt meaningful or timeless?

5. **Presence, Patience, and Renewal**

Building Presence:

- Begin the day with three deep breaths before checking your phone.
- Practice awareness during ordinary moments: when you eat, walk, or listen.
- Work with full attention for short stretches; rest with full permission in between.

Cultivating Patience:

- Set long-term goals with flexible timelines.
- View consistency as progress, even when results are unseen.
- When impatience arises, pause and ask: *What lesson might time be teaching me right now?*

Rhythms of Renewal:

- Protect sleep. It is not lost time but stored energy.
- Schedule unstructured time for creative rest and mental breathing.
- Step away daily for 10–15 minutes of silence, nature, or reflection.

6. **The Weekly Reset Routine**
   - A weekly ritual anchors your rhythm and keeps you in sync with your goals.

   Sunday Evening or Monday Morning Checklist:

   - Review last week's tasks and emotional state.
   - Identify what gave energy and what drained it.
   - Reconnect with your long-term goals.
   - Choose 3 priorities for the upcoming week.
   - Block out focused time for these in your calendar.
   - Plan one act of rest or renewal.
   - Write one affirmation: "I will give my time to what matters most."

7. **The Mindset Reset: Timeless Principles**

   Keep These Reminders Visible:

   - Time is not an enemy to be conquered; it is a teacher to be understood.
   - Busyness is not the same as progress.
   - Your attention shapes the texture of your days.
   - Every pause is part of the rhythm of productivity.

- Energy, not hours, determines the quality of output.
- Simplicity creates focus. Focus creates freedom.
- Patience does not delay progress; it deepens it.
- You cannot manage time. You can only manage the quality of your presence within it.

8. **Monthly Reflection Journal**

- At the end of each month, take 30 minutes to reflect and recalibrate.

Guided Prompts:

- What accomplishments am I most proud of this month?
- What patterns of distraction or energy drain appeared?
- Which habits or practices improved my days?
- How have my priorities evolved?
- What is one thing I will stop doing?
- What is one thing I will do more intentionally next month?

Optional Practice:

Write a brief "Letter to Time" each month. Express what you have learned, where you struggled, and what you hope to experience in the coming weeks. It deepens reflection and strengthens awareness.

9. **Living the Art of Time**

When you finish reading this book, do not look for perfection. Look for rhythm. Life will still move quickly, demands will still appear, and days will still feel crowded. But if you practice awareness, align your time with what matters, and protect your focus, you will begin to live differently. You will no longer feel like time is slipping through your hands. You will begin to experience time as a companion, one that rewards attention, honesty, and presence.

Time is not something to be mastered. It is something to be lived. And living it well begins with one conscious hour at a time.

ꙮ